DOUBLE TAKE!
A New Look at Opposites

Susan Hood

illustrated by Jay Fleck

WALKER STUDIO
AN IMPRINT OF WALKER BOOKS

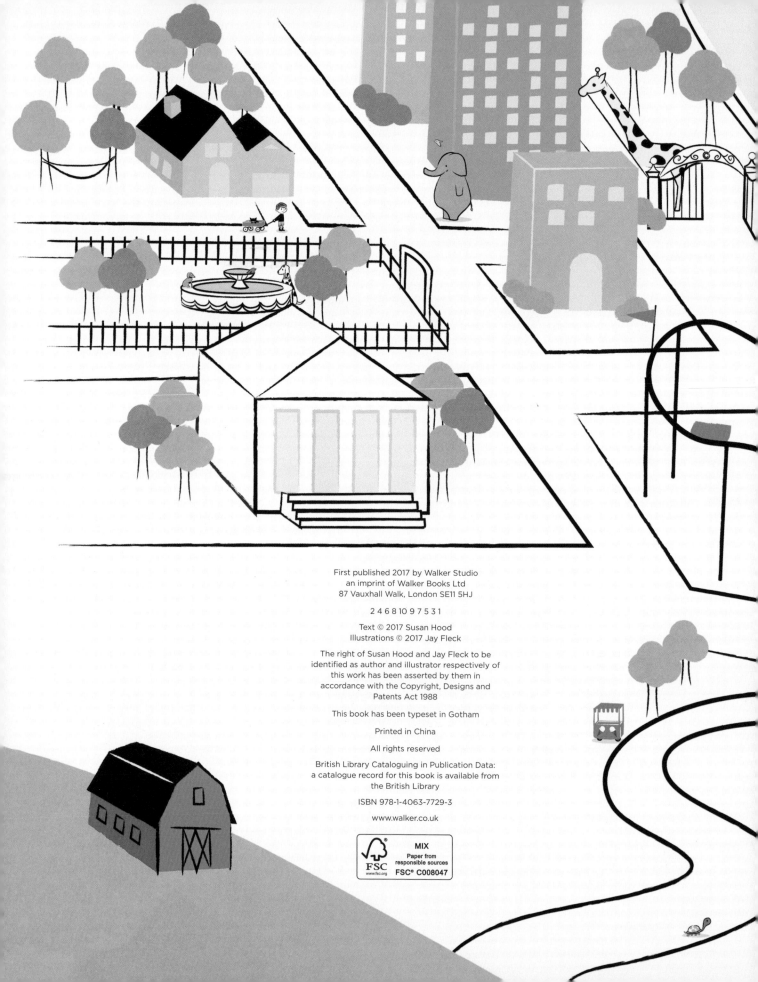

First published 2017 by Walker Studio
an imprint of Walker Books Ltd
87 Vauxhall Walk, London SE11 5HJ

2 4 6 8 10 9 7 5 3 1

Text © 2017 Susan Hood
Illustrations © 2017 Jay Fleck

The right of Susan Hood and Jay Fleck to be
identified as author and illustrator respectively of
this work has been asserted by them in
accordance with the Copyright, Designs and
Patents Act 1988

This book has been typeset in Gotham

Printed in China

British Library Cataloguing in Publication Data:
a catalogue record for this book is available from
the British Library

ISBN 978-1-4063-7729-3

www.walker.co.uk

MIX
Paper from
responsible sources
FSC® C008047
FSC
www.fsc.org

For Emily and Peter, two sides of one heart,
and for all the roads ahead
S. H.

To Suzanne, Audrey and Owen with love
J. F.

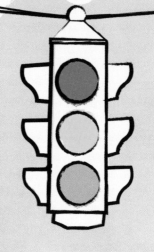

Do you know opposites –
YES or NO?

If I say STOP,
you say GO.

If I say LEFT,

you say RIGHT!

IN?

OUT!

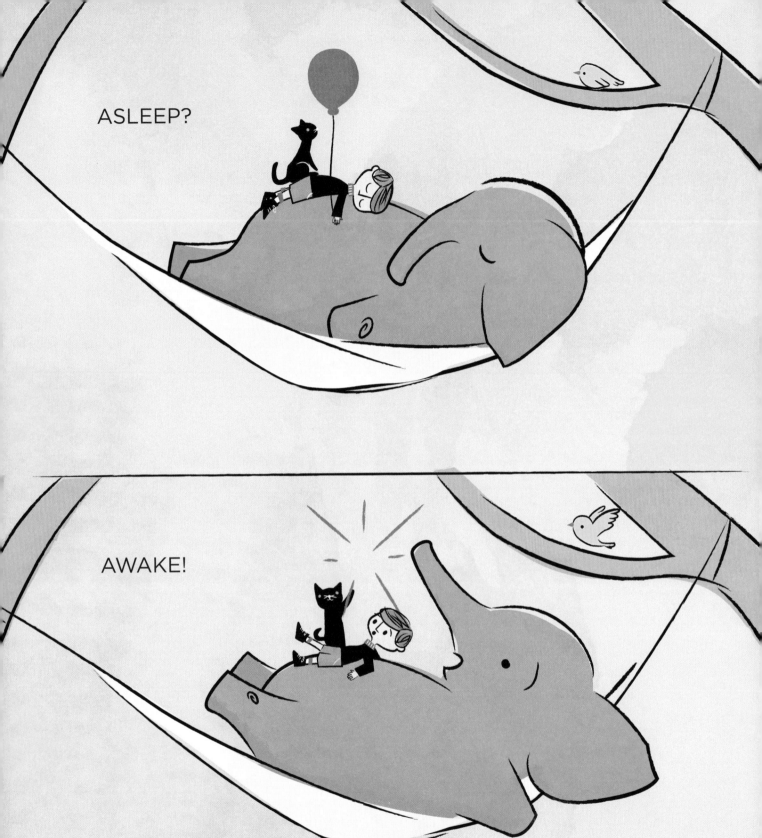

ASLEEP?

AWAKE!

Opposites are a piece of cake!

While those pairs are plain

as DAY ...

and NIGHT,

not every duo is so BLACK and WHITE.

Who knows what is **BIG**

unless there is SMALL?

Does SHORT measure up
except next to TALL?

HIGH might look hazy

until we see LOW.

A racer's called *FAST*

when rivals are S L O W .

Now just when you think you've mastered that notion,
watch relative words set matters in motion.

Who's NEAR   and   who's FAR

couldn't be clearer,

but ...

does
NEAR
become
FAR

when FAR flies in NEARer?

Who's **STRONG**

and who's WEAK
is hardly perplexing.

But **STRONG** can look WEAK when a **new champ** is flexing!

Point of view (where you are)
can affect what you see.
Go in close. Then back up –
you'll see differently!

These dashes and dots
in a rainbow array ...

can paint a new picture when you step away!

Who is AHEAD
and who is BEHIND ...

is different for everyone standing in line.

What is ABOVE

and what is BELOW?

The answer depends on who wants to know.

A careless assumption can be a mistake.
Look once, then again;
do a quick double take!

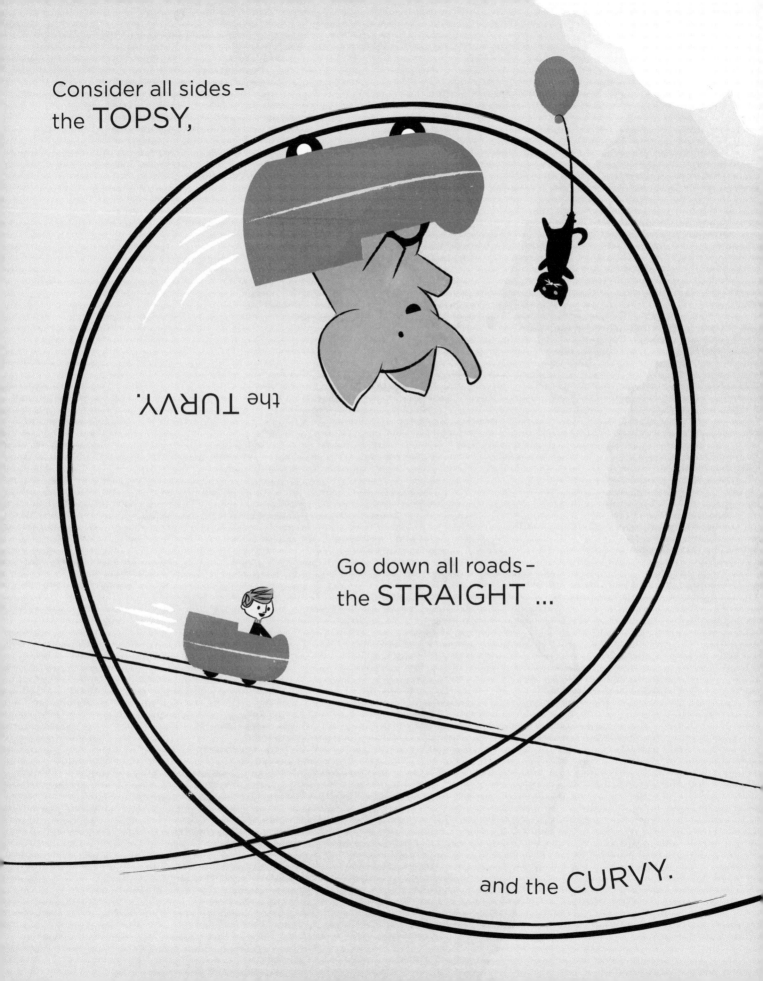

Consider all sides –
the TOPSY,

the TURVY.

Go down all roads –
the STRAIGHT ...

and the CURVY.

Turn things around! Give them a twist.
FIND a new view
        that you might have MISSED!

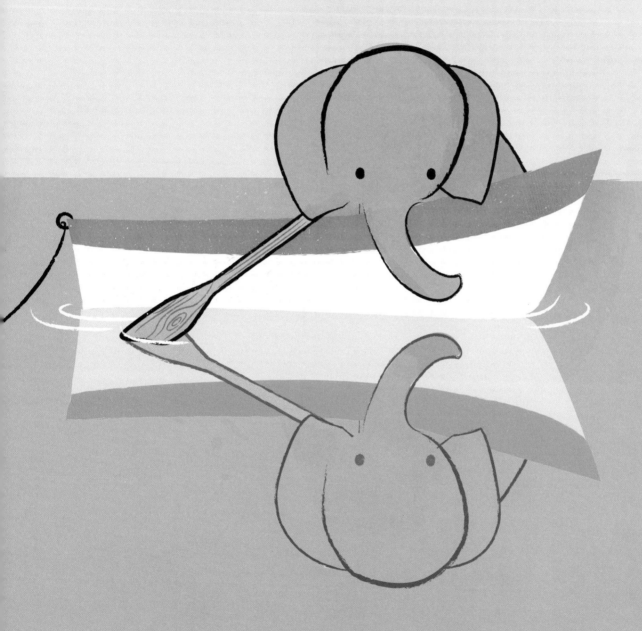

A brand-new direction, a closer inspection,
might lead to reflection and maybe ...

perfection.